MIDFIELDER

Michael Hurley

www.raintreepublishers.co.uk
Visit our website to find out more information about Raintree books.

To order:
☎ Phone 0845 6044371
📄 Fax +44 (0) 1865 312263
📠 Email myorders@raintreepublishers.co.uk

Customers from outside the UK please telephone +44 1865 312262

Raintree is an imprint of Capstone Global Library Limited, a company incorporated in England and Wales having its registered office at 7 Pilgrim Street, London, EC4V 6LB – Registered company number: 6695582

Edited by Louise Galpine, Vaarunika Dharmapala, and John-Paul Wilkins
Designed by Philippa Jenkins
Original illustrations © Capstone Global Library Ltd 2010
Illustrated by KJA-artists.com
Picture research by Hannah Taylor
Originated by Capstone Global Library Ltd
Printed and bound in China by Leo Paper Products Ltd

ISBN 978 1 406216 41 7 (hardback)
14 13 12 11 10
10 9 8 7 6 5 4 3 2 1

ISBN 978 1406217 41 4 (paperback)
15 14 13 12 11
10 9 8 7 6 5 4 3 2 1

British Library Cataloguing in Publication Data
Hurley, Michael
Midfielder. -- (Football files)
796.3'342-dc22
A full catalogue record for this book is available from the British Library.

Acknowledgements
We would like to thank the following for permission to reproduce photographs: Action Images pp. **6**, **14** (MSI), **22** (Flash Press), **27** (The FA/Paul Harding); Corbis pp. **7** (Victor Fraile), **8** (Reuters/Dan Chung), **19** (Reuters/Nigel Roddis), **21** (epa/Ballesteros); Getty Images pp. **16** (Jerry Cooke) **24** (Darren Walsh), **29** (Robert Clanflone); © KPT Power Photos **background image**; Press Association pp. **5** (Empics/Matthew Impey), **15** (Empics/Peter Robinson), **18**, **23** (Empics/Matthew Ashton); Reuters pp. **10** (Nigel Roddis), **11** (Phil Noble), **12** (Toby Melville), Shutterstock **background image** (© Nikola I), **22 inset** (© R-O-M-A).

Cover photograph of Liverpool's Steven Gerrard during a Chelsea vs Liverpool match, 10 February 2008, reproduced with permission of Corbis/NewSport/Professional Sport/ Stephen Wake.

We would like to thank Dr Sarah Schenker for her invaluable help in the preparation of this book.

Every effort has been made to contact copyright holders of material reproduced in this book. Any omissions will be rectified in subsequent printings if notice is given to the publisher.

CONTENTS

Some words are shown in bold, **like this**. You can find out what they mean by looking in the glossary on page 30.

BEING A MIDFIELDER

People all over the world enjoy playing and watching football. It is a sport that anyone can take part in because you don't need expensive equipment or a special place to play. All you need is something to use as a ball, some friends, and a patch of ground.

Many countries in the world have **professional** football **leagues**. The players in the leagues get paid to play and their fans pay to watch them. The leagues are organized by national football associations.

Organized football matches have two teams with eleven players on each side. Each team is made up of players who have different positions and roles on the pitch. A team will usually have two central midfielders and two wide midfielders, one of each on the left and the right of the pitch. Central midfielders will help their team in defence and attack, with individuals choosing to focus their attention on one or the other. Wide midfielders, sometimes called wingers, are usually attackers.

All midfielders need to have excellent **stamina**. A defensive midfielder needs to be strong, good at **tackling**, **marking**, and passing. An attacking midfielder needs to be skilful, good at passing, and shooting. Wide midfielders need **pace** and are expected to be able to **dribble**, pass, and **cross**.

Cesc Fabregas, one of the most exciting midfielders in the world, uses his strength and skill to hold off Portsmouth's Aaron Mokoena.

DAVID BECKHAM

David Beckham is one of the most famous and recognizable footballers in the world. Beckham grew up in London and moved to Manchester when he joined Manchester United as a young player. He signed his first contract with the club in 1991, on his 14th birthday. A year later, he was part of a very strong and skilful Manchester United youth team. They won the 1992 FA Youth Cup. This was the first success of Beckham's amazing career.

David Beckham (front row, middle) began his career at Manchester United by winning the FA Youth Cup in 1992.

Playing for Manchester United

Beckham made his Manchester United **debut** as a **substitute** in a **League** Cup match in 1992. In 1995, he made his Premier League debut in a match against fierce rivals Leeds United. In Beckham's first season Manchester United won the league and the FA Cup. Beckham was beginning to become an important player for his club. He started to show how good he was at taking **free kicks** and **corners**. His accuracy from these **set pieces** helped his team to score lots of goals. In his second season with Manchester United Beckham scored an amazing goal. He shot from the half-way line and the ball flew over the **opposition goalkeeper** and into the net. It was an outstanding show of skill.

Beckham enjoyed another career highlight in 1999. Manchester United won the league, FA Cup, and **UEFA** Champions League all in the same year. Beckham was an essential part of Manchester United's success. He was a regular in the team and helped to create and score lots of goals during the season. He was rewarded with the runner-up position in the World and European Player of the Year Awards.

Playing for Real Madrid

After 14 years at Manchester United Beckham transferred to Real Madrid in Spain. Beckham had to adjust to living in a new country and playing with new teammates. Beckham's time with Madrid was not as successful as the time he spent with Manchester United, but he did win one league title in 2007. He was crucial to this success and his set pieces and hard work were appreciated by his teammates and fans. After four years in Spain, Beckham moved to LA Galaxy in the United States. He has also played for AC Milan, in Italy.

David Beckham prepares to take a free kick for Real Madrid. Beckham's accuracy from set pieces helped Real Madrid win the Spanish league title in 2007.

Playing for England

Beckham started his international career with England in 1996. He has played at three World Cup tournaments for England. He was the England captain at the World Cup in 2002 and in 2006. In 2009 he broke the record for the highest number of England international appearances for an **outfield player**. Beckham has had to deal with a lot of pressure during his career because people's expectations of him are so high.

David Beckham salutes fans as England defeats Argentina in a World Cup finals match in 2002.

Services to football

In 2003 Beckham was awarded an OBE (Order of the British Empire) by the Queen for his services to football.

SWERVING THE BALL

David Beckham can strike the ball powerfully and accurately. When Beckham takes a free kick he is able to swerve the ball. This makes it difficult for the goalkeeper to make a save. The most famous free kick that Beckham scored from was against Greece in 2001. He scored to draw the match 2–2 and make sure England made it to the 2002 World Cup.

1. The player prepares to strike, keeping her balance, with her eyes on the ball.

2. The player keeps her head over the ball and uses the side of her foot to make contact with it.

3. She keeps her balance and makes powerful contact with the ball. Using the side of her foot will make the ball move from right to left.

Charity in football

David Beckham is one of the most recognizable sportsmen in the world. Footballers like Beckham who achieve such a high level of success and fame can use their celebrity status to influence other people's lives positively.

In 2002 he started a charity with his wife, called the David and Victoria Beckham Children's Charity. It has raised money to buy wheelchairs and other equipment for the children who need them.

Beckham was made a **UNICEF** ambassador in 2005. As part of this role, he spent time at a health clinic in Sierra Leone, West Africa, in 2008. UNICEF works to help children affected by malaria, diarrhoea, and malnutrition, as well as diseases such as measles and tuberculosis.

Steven Gerrard was invited to join the Liverpool Academy when he was nine years old. The coaches at Liverpool recognized that Gerrard was very talented and would have a bright future as a footballer. The coaches helped him to become a better player as he got older. He played in the youth team and then in the **reserves**.

Here, Steven Gerrard is in action for Liverpool in an English Premier League match in 2008.

Playing for Liverpool

In the summer of 1997 Gerrard signed a **professional** contract at Liverpool. Several months later he made his **debut** for the club. He came on as a **substitute** in a match against Blackburn Rovers. A week later he started his first **league** match as a Liverpool player versus Tottenham Hotspur.

As a young player Gerrard played in a lot of different positions. It soon became clear that his best position was in central midfield. He has all the qualities that a world-class midfielder needs. He can **tackle**, pass, shoot, and **dribble**. He is quick and he is good at **headers**. On top of his technical skills Gerrard is also a leader on the pitch. He always appears to be totally committed and determined.

Steven Gerrard became Liverpool captain in 2004. Here, he shows very good technique as he strikes the ball.

Steven Gerrard (centre) and Andorra's Marcio Vieira (left) fight for the ball during a World Cup 2010 qualifying match in 2009.

Liverpool had an incredible year in 2001. They won the FA Cup, League Cup, and the **UEFA** Cup. Gerrard was an important part of this success and he was named the Professional Footballer's Association (PFA) Young Player of the Year. Liverpool won the UEFA Champions League in 2005 and the FA Cup again in 2006. Gerrard's performances and goals were very important for Liverpool. In the Champions League final Liverpool were 3–0 down at half time against AC Milan. In the second half Gerrard scored and helped to inspire his team to draw 3–3. In the end, Liverpool won the match on **penalties**.

Gerrard also inspired his team's success in the FA Cup final. He scored twice in the match. His second goal was a powerful shot from about 27 metres (30 yards) out. Liverpool won the final on penalties. Gerrard was awarded the 2006 PFA Player of the Year award for his brilliant, **consistent** performances.

Record breaker!

Steven Gerrard has scored 29 goals for Liverpool in European competitions, which is a record in the club's history.

Playing for England

Gerrard has been an important player for England since he made his debut in 2000. He has now played more than 70 times for his country. He has scored some important and spectacular goals. Gerrard scored his first goal for England in a match against Germany in 2001. Unfortunately, he missed the opportunity to play for England at the 2002 World Cup because of an injury.

LONG-RANGE SHOOTING

Gerrard is well known for his long-range shooting ability. He has very good **technique** when it comes to striking a ball. When shooting from a distance, try to keep your head over the ball as you strike it. This should stop the ball going too high in the air and over the goal.

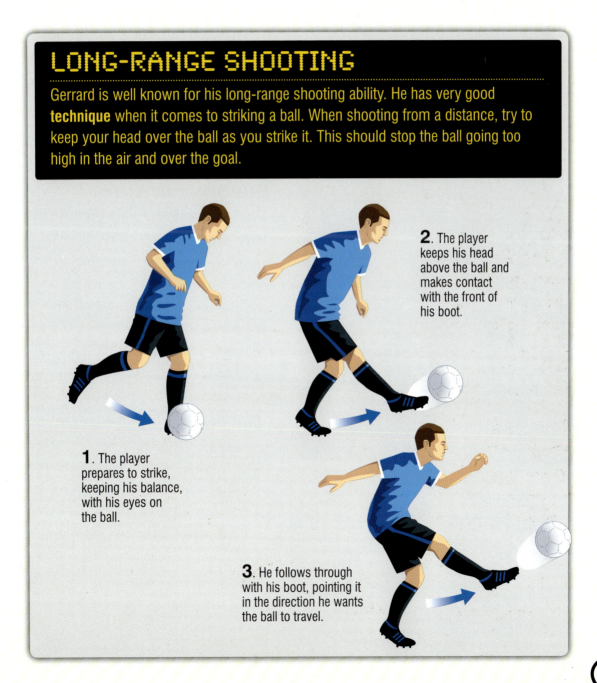

2. The player keeps his head above the ball and makes contact with the front of his boot.

1. The player prepares to strike, keeping his balance, with his eyes on the ball.

3. He follows through with his boot, pointing it in the direction he wants the ball to travel.

JOHAN CRUYFF

Johan Cruyff was an attacking midfielder who played in the 1960s, 70s, and 80s. He was born in Amsterdam, in the Netherlands, and began his career with his local football club, Ajax. He grew up living very close to the Ajax stadium and his mother worked there as a cleaner. Cruyff made his **debut** for Ajax in 1964, when he was 17 years old. He was a very talented young player. He could **dribble** the ball and pass it accurately. He could also score goals. Cruyff was lucky that he was in a team with other very good footballers.

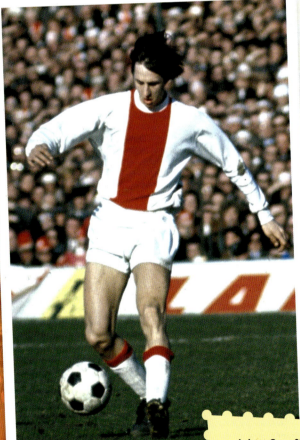

Success at Ajax

Cruyff helped Ajax win the **league** title six times in the next ten years. They also won the Dutch Cup four times. The most exciting and successful period for Ajax was in the early 1970s. With Cruyff in their team they won the **UEFA** European Cup (now Champions League) three times in a row between 1971 and 1973. This was an incredible achievement. Cruyff was the most important player in a very talented team. During this period, he played in 318 matches and scored an amazing 250 goals. He won the European Footballer of the Year Award in 1971 and 1973.

Johan Cruyff dribbles the ball while playing for Ajax in 1971.

Playing for Barcelona

In 1973 Cruyff left Ajax to join Barcelona, in Spain. In his first season he helped the team win the league title. He won the European Footballer of the Year Award for the third time at the end of his first season with Barcelona. Unfortunately for Cruyff, he won only one more trophy while he was at Barcelona, when they won the Spanish Cup in 1978. He retired from football soon after.

Health and fitness

Johan Cruyff used to be a heavy smoker. This was not unusual in the 1970s, but these days people know much more about the dangers of smoking. Footballers need to stay as healthy as possible. Smoking can damage a footballer's performance on the field, making him short of breath. It can also lead to many diseases such as cancer, heart disease, and lung disease.

Here, Johan Cruyff is in action for Barcelona. He is one of the greatest footballers in the Spanish club's history.

Comeback

Cruyff was not retired for long. He made his comeback in the United States in 1979, playing for Los Angeles Aztecs. He later played for Washington Diplomats as well. In 1981 Cruyff returned to Spain to play for one season for a small club called Levante. He then moved back to Ajax and helped them to win the league twice in a row. Cruyff finished his career at Feyenoord in the Netherlands. He was part of the team that won the Dutch league title in 1984. At the age of 36 he managed to play in 33 league matches for Feyenoord and scored 11 goals.

Johan Cruyff (middle) celebrates with his teammates after scoring a goal for the Netherlands in 1974.

THE CRUYFF TURN

Johan Cruyff invented his own move on the pitch, which became known as the "Cruyff turn". He would begin by moving in one direction with the ball, then he would drag it behind himself and move in another direction. **Opposition** players often did not know where the ball had gone.

1. The attacker (in red) looks as though he is going to pass the ball. Instead, he flicks it back with the inside of his foot.

2. The attacker turns quickly, losing his opponent.

3. The attacker turns turns into the space left by his opponent. He has successfully kept possession of the ball.

CRISTIANO RONALDO

Cristiano Ronaldo was born in Madeira, a small island off the coast of Portugal. He began playing football for his local amateur team when he was eight years old. When he was twelve he moved to Portugal to play for Sporting Lisbon.

Ronaldo scored two goals on his **debut** for the club. The supporters were very happy to see a skilful young winger on their team. Ronaldo's first season with Sporting Lisbon ended with the **league** title. At the end of the season Ronaldo represented Portugal in the **UEFA** Under 17 European Championship. He was one of the outstanding players during the tournament and he attracted interest from some of the biggest football clubs in Europe. Manchester United signed Ronaldo for a huge fee of over £12 million. It was a lot of money for a young player with little experience.

While he was at Sporting Lisbon, Cristiano Ronaldo caught the eye with his skill and dribbling ability.

Playing for Manchester United

Ronaldo made his debut for Manchester United in the Premier League in 2003. It was a very memorable debut for the young player. He only played for the last 30 minutes of the match but he made an immediate impact. He dazzled the **opposition** defence with his **pace** and **dribbling** ability. He managed to set up two goals in a 4–0 win over Bolton.

Ronaldo followed this amazing debut performance with some inconsistent performances. Over the next two seasons Ronaldo had to improve his decision-making on the pitch and his all round ability as a footballer.

Health and fitness

Cristiano Ronaldo does not drink alcohol. Drinking too much alcohol can affect a player's fitness and cause dehydration. Most footballers these days either avoid alcohol or drink very little of it.

Recognition

In 2007 Manchester United won the league title for the first time in four years. Cristiano Ronaldo was one of their best and most **consistent** players. Ronaldo was named the Professional Football Association's Young Player of the Year and also their Player of the Year. He was only the second player in history to win both awards at the same time.

The following season was another very successful one for Ronaldo. He scored over 40 goals and was named the European and World Footballer of the Year. He was rewarded for his outstanding performances for Manchester United in the league and in the Champions League. Manchester United won the Premier League for the second year in a row. They beat Chelsea in the final of the Champions League. In Ronaldo's final season with Manchester United they won the league title again. They also got to the Champions League final but were beaten by a very good Barcelona team.

THE RONALDO STEP-OVER

Cristiano Ronaldo is known for his step-overs. This means confusing the opposition players by pretending to kick the ball as he runs with it. Sometimes Ronaldo performs several step-overs in a row, leaving **opponents** guessing where he's going next.

1. Running with the ball, the attacker (in red) looks as though he is going to pass.

2. Instead of passing, he lifts his foot above the ball, tricking his opponent.

3. The attacker then uses the outside of his other foot to move the ball and run in the opposite direction.

Cristiano Ronaldo during his transfer to Real Madrid. Around 80,000 fans turned up to celebrate when he joined the club.

An expensive footballer

Cristiano Ronaldo is the most expensive footballer in the world. In 2009 he moved from Manchester United to Real Madrid for £80 million. This broke the football world transfer record. Real Madrid held the previous records. They signed Kaka from AC Milan for around £56 million and before that Zinedine Zidane from Juventus for around £46 million.

CLAUDE MAKELELE

Claude Makelele was born in the Democratic Republic of Congo (then known as Zaire) in Africa. He moved to France at the age of four and grew up in Paris. When he was 16 years old he was signed by the French club team Brest. He moved to the north west of France but struggled to adapt to his new surroundings. He was very young and it was the first time he had lived away from his family. He played in the Brest academy for two years before he transferred to Nantes, another French club team.

Makelele soon became an important part of the Nantes team. He played for them for five years and won one **league** title. The team also made it to the Champions League semi-finals in 1996. Makelele transferred to Marseille in southern France in 1997 and spent a year playing for them. He was then signed by Celta Vigo in Spain. He enjoyed a successful period in the Celta midfield and was soon attracting interest from bigger teams.

Here, Claude Makelele is in action for Nantes. He won the French league title with the club in 1995.

Claude Makelele (left) wins the ball in midfield with help from teammate Luis Figo.

Playing for Real Madrid

In 2000 Makelele signed with Real Madrid and immediately improved their team. He helped to make them solid and harder than ever to beat. His simple style of play involved **tackling** or **intercepting** the ball from the **opposition** and then passing the ball to his more technically gifted teammates. Madrid enjoyed a lot of success with Makelele in central midfield. He helped them to win two league titles and the **UEFA** Champions League.

Playing for Chelsea and beyond

Although he was an important part of Madrid's success, Makelele was one of their lowest paid players. However, his luck soon changed when, in 2003, Chelsea signed him for around £16.5 million. At Chelsea Makelele enjoyed more success. In his second season he helped the team to win the league for the first time in 50 years. They also won the League Cup. Chelsea went on to win the league again the following year.

In 2008 Makelele's **consistent** performances helped Chelsea to make it to their first ever Champions League final. They lost the final on **penalties** to Manchester United. This was Makelele's last match for Chelsea. He moved to PSG (Paris Saint-Germain) in France where he is expected to finish his outstanding career.

Claude Makelele (right) holds the Premier League trophy as he celebrates winning the English Premier League with his Chelsea teammates.

Playing for France

Makelele made his **debut** for France in 1995. However, he missed out on sharing France's World Cup win in 1998. He had failed to make the **squad**. Since then, however, he has become one of the most dependable and consistent players for France. Makelele has played 71 times for his country. He was part of the team that lost in the final of the 2006 World Cup.

ONE AND TWO TOUCH

Claude Makelele is famous for his ability to successfully pass the ball to a teammate. Central midfield players have to be able to control the ball when they receive it. They must then pass quickly and accurately, making sure they don't lose the ball to the opposition.

1. The player receives the ball and controls it with one touch.

2. The player passes the ball to a teammate with the second touch.

TIPS FOR MIDFIELDERS

Long-range passing

Long-range passing can help teams when they are defending or attacking. If you are defending and you **intercept** the ball, a long pass to a teammate can relieve pressure on the defence. If you are attacking, an accurate long-range pass to a teammate can lead to a goal-scoring opportunity.

Dribbling

Not all midfielders are good at dribbling the ball, but it is a very useful skill to have. Wingers are expected to be able to dribble well. If you can dribble the ball you may cause the opposition to foul you when they try to steal possession of the ball. If you are fouled then your team will receive a free kick or a penalty. Practise running with the ball at your feet. Try dribbling in a straight line, then try dribbling and changing direction.

Short-range passing

All midfielders must be able to pass accurately. Passing over a short distance to a teammate means that your team is more likely to keep possession of the ball. It is important to keep your eyes on the ball and decide which direction you want the ball to go. You must be able to judge the speed of your pass so that it reaches your teammate.

This group of footballers are practising their short-range passing.

Heading

Midfielders should be good at heading the ball. When you practise your headers make sure that you keep your eyes on the ball. You should also try to time your jump so that you connect with the ball accurately. When you make contact with the ball, try to use your forehead. When you get better at headers, try heading the ball in different directions. Remember that if you close your eyes before you connect with the ball, it might not go where you want it to!

Tackling

Midfielders should be able to tackle well. It is an important skill to learn. When you make a tackle, keep your eyes on the ball and try to stay on your feet. If you do not time your tackle correctly you will miss the ball and probably foul the opposition player, giving away a free kick.

Shooting

Often midfielders are a long way from the goal when they shoot. When shooting from a long distance, remember to keep your balance, keep your eye on the ball, and try to strike through the ball in a straight line.

When you are practising your shooting, make sure you keep your eyes on the ball as you strike it.

GLOSSARY

consistent always the same

corner kick taken by the attacking team from the corner of the pitch after the defending team has knocked the ball over the goal line

cross kicking the ball from one side of the pitch to a player in the middle, usually near the goal

debut first time that a player plays for a team

dribble run with the ball

free kick kick of the ball awarded by the referee after a foul

goalkeeper position of a player on the pitch. The goalkeeper guards the goal and is the only player allowed to touch the ball with his hands.

header when you connect with the ball using your head

intercept getting to the ball before an opposition player

league group of teams that play against each other during the football season. There are national football leagues all over the world.

mark keep close to an opponent to try to stop them getting the ball

opponent/opposition person or team that you are playing against

outfield player any player on the pitch except the goalkeeper

pace speed. A player with lots of pace can move around the pitch quickly.

penalty the referee gives a penalty if a foul happens in the 18-yard box. The ball is placed on a spot 12 yards (10.9 metres) from the goal and only the goalkeeper is allowed to stop the shot.

professional being paid a salary to play football

reserve back-up players who do not play in the first team

set pieces when the ball is delivered from a standing position after a pause in play. Free kicks and corners are set pieces.

squad group of players from which a team is chosen. A squad is usually made up of around 20–25 players from which a team of 11 is chosen.

stamina ability to take part in physical activity for a long time

substitute player who does not start a match but who can replace a player on the pitch. Three substitutes can be used in most matches.

tackle take the ball from an opponent by using your feet

technique way of doing something. For a midfielder there is a good and bad technique for passing the ball.

UEFA (Union of European Football Associations) organization responsible for European football

UNICEF (United Nations Children's Fund) organization that works for children's health, rights, and protection around the world

FIND OUT MORE

Books to read

Usborne Activities: 50 Soccer Skills, Jonathan Sheikh-Miller (Usborne, 2008)

Essential Sports: Football, Andy Smith (Heinemann Library, 2008)

Sport Files: Wayne Rooney, John Townsend (Raintree, 2009)

The World Cup series, Michael Hurley (Heinemann Library, 2009)

Websites

http://www.thefa.com/skills

The website of the English Football Association. This site has lots of videos to help you improve your skills and technique.

http://news.bbc.co.uk/sport2/hi/academy/default.stm

The BBC Sport Academy website includes videos and tutorials to help you learn more about playing football.

http://www.fifa.com/aboutfifa/developing/medical/playerhealth.html

The FIFA website has information about how to get the most out of playing football by eating healthily and avoiding injuries.

INDEX